15666 EN
Vostok 1: Fi **W9-BGI-279**

Cole, Michael D.
ATOS BL 5.5
Points: 1.0   MG

COUNTDOWN TO SPACE

VOSTOK I
First Human in Space

Michael D. Cole

Series Advisor:
John E. McLeaish
Chief, Public Information Office, retired,
NASA Johnson Space Center

Enslow Publishers, Inc.

40 Industrial Road	PO Box 38
Box 398	Aldershot
Berkeley Heights, NJ 07922	Hants GU12 6BP
USA	UK

http://www.enslow.com

Library of Congress Cataloging-in-Publication Data

Cole, Michael D.
    Vostok 1: first human in space / Michael D. Cole.
        p. cm. — (Countdown to space)
    Includes bibliographical references and index.
    ISBN 0-89490-541-4
    1. Gagarin, Îùrii Alekseevich, 1934–1968—Juvenile literature. 2. Astronauts—
Soviet Union—Biography—Juvenile literature. 3. Vostok (Spacecraft)—Juvenile
literature. [1. Gagarin, Yuri Alekseyevich, 1934–1968. 2. Astronauts.] I.Title.
II. Series: Cole, Michael D. Countdown to space.
TL789.85.G3C65 1995
629.45' 0092—dc20
[B]   94-41180
                                              CIP
                                              AC

Printed in the U.S.A.

10 9 8 7 6 5 4

Illustration Credits:
Itar-Tass/Sovfoto, pp. 8, 34, 36; Ria-Novosti/Sovfoto, pp. 24, 28; Russian
Information Office, pp. 4, 17, 23, 30, 35, 37, 39; Sovfoto/Eastfoto, pp. 7, 9,
10, 11, 15, 19, 31.

Cover Illustration:
Sovfoto/Eastfoto (foreground); © L. Manning/Westlight (background).

CONTENTS

Soviet cosmonaut Yuri Gagarin was the first human in space.

Pioneer to Space

"Yuri, it's time to get up."

The doctor had no trouble waking Yuri Gagarin in the early morning of April 12, 1961.

"How did you sleep?" the doctor asked.

"As I was taught to," Gagarin said with a smile.[1] The twenty-seven-year-old Soviet pilot was eager for what lay ahead that day. He was about to live a pilot's dream. Today he would attempt to fly where no human being had flown before.

The huge white Vostok rocket sat at the Tyuratum launch site in the Soviet Union. In a few hours Gagarin would climb aboard the rocket and blast off from the launchpad. If all went well, he would become the first human being to fly into space and orbit Earth.

Yuri Gagarin was a Russian who served his country

as a Soviet cosmonaut. He and his fellow cosmonauts had been training for spaceflight for more than a year. They prepared at a special training center in northwestern Russia called Zvezdniy Gorodok. In Russian that means "Star City."

Gagarin was not named to make the historic first flight until April 8, 1961, just four days earlier. The Soviet space program was now ready to rocket their first cosmonaut into space.

After Gagarin ate breakfast, several sensors were attached to his body. They would monitor his heartbeat, breathing, and other bodily functions during the flight. Then Gagarin and his backup pilot, Gherman Titov, were helped into their spacesuits.

The suits included a special pair of long underwear that fit over the biosensors. Next came the pressure suit to protect Gagarin or Titov in case the cabin of the spacecraft failed. Then they stepped into some bright orange coveralls. The color would help the recovery team spot the cosmonaut after he landed.

Finally came the gloves, boots, and the large white helmet. Just above the helmet's visor were the large letters CCCP in red. These letters of the Russian alphabet would translate to USSR in the English alphabet. The letters stood for Union of Soviet Socialist Republics. Gagarin and Titov were now ready for the drive to the waiting spacecraft. The countdown had already begun.

A bus carried Gagarin, Titov, and other support people to the launchpad. After the short ride, Gagarin stepped from the bus. He was met with emotional applause from the large team of technicians and engineers working at the launchpad. He shook hands and exchanged hugs with many of the people waiting at the foot of the rocket.[2]

Then he climbed awkwardly up the steep metal

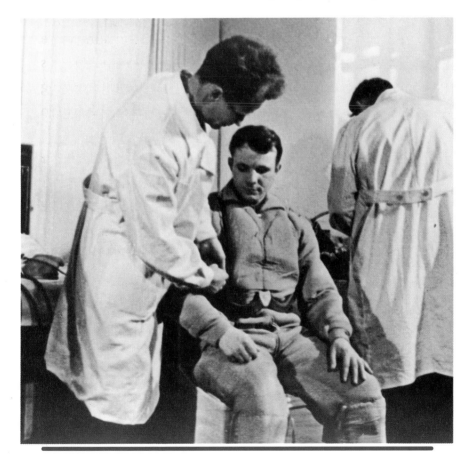

Gagarin is checked by doctors before his spaceflight on April 12, 1961.

Yuri Gagarin waves to the crowd before entering the elevator which would take him up to Vostok 1.

staircase leading to the elevator. He turned and waved to the crowd of engineers, Soviet government officials, and military officers below. Before he stepped into the elevator with the rocket's chief designer, Gagarin said a few words.

"At this instant, the whole of my life seems to be condensed into one wonderful moment," he said. "Of course I am happy. In all times . . . the greatest happiness for man has been to take part in new discoveries. To be the first to enter the cosmos, to engage single-handed in an unprecedented duel with nature—could one dream of anything more!"[3]

Gagarin then said good-bye and stepped into the elevator. He was at the top of the rocket in moments. Gagarin squeezed through the hatch and into the spacecraft. He and the rocket's chief designer, Sergei Korolev, spent more than an hour alone at the top of the rocket. Then Korolev left and the hatch was sealed. Korolev came down in the elevator. Gagarin was now left alone to face the dangers ahead.

"Attention Earth," Gagarin said, "this is the cosmonaut. Radio connection tested. Initial position of switch on guidance system panel correct. Globe in

Before the flight of Vostok 1, *Yuri Gagarin (left) talks with Sergei Korolev (right), the spaceship's chief designer.*

Minutes before liftoff, Vostok 1 *rests on the launchpad.*

starting position. . . . Am feeling fine. Ready for liftoff."[4]

Another hour passed as Gagarin waited in *Vostok 1.* The countdown was delayed while a faulty valve was repaired. Soon the countdown resumed and the historic moment approached. Gagarin heard the final commands on the radio headset in his helmet.

"Switch to Go position!" said a voice from the control room.

"Air purging! Idle run!" said another. The fuel tower disconnected and slowly backed away from the rocket.

"Ignition!" The power cable arm swung away. The spacecraft was now on internal power. It was free of all connections to the launch towers. The rocket and Yuri Gagarin were ready for humanity's first flight into space.

Flames of red and white flashed out from the rocket's huge engines. Gagarin heard the engine's roar and felt the rocket slowly lift from the pad.

"Liftoff!" Gagarin heard from the control room. The rocket lifted slowly at first. Then it cleared the pad. The powerful engines roared on and the spacecraft was soon soaring into the sky.

"Off we go!" Gagarin said with excitement.[5]

The rocket accelerated rapidly as it climbed

With a blaze of fire, Vostok 1 *takes off on its historic flight.*

through the sky. The engines continued their mighty thrust, winning their fight with the force of gravity. The acceleration pressed Gagarin deeper and deeper into his couch. The sensation felt like hundreds of pounds were pushing down on him. These are called G forces or G loads.

The spacecraft pushed on until the rocket's four strap-on boosters separated. Only the main booster was left to thrust him into orbit.

"The fairing has been discarded," Gagarin said. "I see the Earth. The loads are increasing. Feeling fine."[6] The spacecraft rocketed onward until the main engine shut down. Normally when the acceleration stopped, he would be thrown forward against the straps. But this time was different.

This time Gagarin felt his body floating up off his seat. He was suspended in the air against his seat harness. Everything around him that was not fastened down began to float in the cabin.

He was in space! He and *Vostok 1* were in orbit around Earth.

Gagarin looked out his window for the first time. He became the first person to see with his own eyes the spherical shape of his own planet. Yuri Gagarin realized he was indeed the first human being in space.

2

Gagarin in Orbit

Radio broadcasts sent a wave of excitement through the city of Moscow.

"The Soviet Union has successfully launched a manned spaceship-satellite into an orbit around Earth. Present aboard the spaceship is the pilot-cosmonaut, Yuri Alexeivich Gagarin, an Air Force pilot, twenty-seven years of age!"[1]

The launch was made at 9:07 A.M. Moscow time. The radio announcement sent the people of the city cheering into the streets.

A correspondent reported, "Crowds in Red Square and Sverdlov Square, groups marching up Gorky street . . . shoppers huddling in the stores—everyone is talking about Yuri Gagarin."[2]

All of the Soviet Union gathered around their radios

to listen to reports of Gagarin's flight. Gagarin's wife, Valya, had heard the news that her husband was in space. She too listened to the reports with both worry and excitement. Her apartment was soon full of neighbors. Gagarin's daughters, two-year-old Yelena, and two-month-old Galina, were near their mother as she recorded the events in a school notebook. She brushed tears from her face as she listened to the reports of her husband's voyage.[3]

Gagarin was travelling faster than any human had flown before. He orbited at 17,400 miles per hour over Siberia and Japan.[4] Gagarin grew used to the sensation of being weightless. At the same time he reported instrument readings and checked his equipment.

"Flight proceeds well," he said. "Instruments are functioning excellently . . . feeling fine . . . the machine is functioning normally."[5]

Gagarin's spacecraft, the *Vostok*, was shaped like a sphere, with another cone-shaped module attached to the bottom. Gagarin sat in a special couch in the spherical part. The couch was designed to eject itself and Gagarin from the ship during the landing sequence. The spacecraft and Gagarin would then parachute to the ground separately.

The cone-shaped module contained the reentry engine. This engine would slow the spacecraft for its reentry into Earth's atmosphere. After the engine fired, it would drop away. Only the spherical part of the ship would reenter the atmosphere.

Yuri Gagarin reads to his two daughters, Galina (left) and Yelena (right). At the time of Gagarin's flight, his daughters were with their mother and friends at home.

Gagarin made his observations of the Earth through a circular porthole in front of him. These observations were of great interest to the Russian people. They were listening to official reports of his progress on Soviet radio.

"The sky looks very, very dark and the Earth is bluish," he said.[6] Gagarin could easily see the shores of continents and islands. He could follow great rivers and distinguish mountains and hills. Over Russia he could see the big squares of the farm fields. He could even tell which fields were plowed and which were planted.

Gagarin observed that the sun appeared many times brighter when seen from space. The stars also appeared brighter and clearer. As his voyage continued, the sun began to set over the Earth's horizon behind him. He was entering the Earth's shadow, the night side of the Earth.

Gagarin watched the sun set over a bright blue band across the horizon. The band quickly turned to orange. Then, suddenly, it was dark. Nothing was visible. He was over the Atlantic Ocean at that moment. It was some time before he passed over land and made out the lights of large towns.

Vostok 1 flew on. Gagarin practiced eating and drinking in space. The weightlessness caused him no discomfort. To test his hand-eye coordination, he practiced handwriting. He had to hold the writing pad to keep it from floating away. Gagarin thought it felt strange to write with a hand that was weightless.[7] But otherwise there was no change in his writing.

During the entire mission, Gagarin never needed to touch the controls to pilot the spacecraft. The designers of the ship wanted the cosmonauts to fly in the spacecraft only as passengers. During their training, Yuri and his fellow cosmonauts protested. They were pilots, and they wanted the ability to control the ship if the ground systems failed. Because of their protests, a manual back-up system was added.

Soviet cosmonauts who commanded various Vostok *missions (from left to right): Gherman Titov, Yuri Gagarin, Valentina Tereshkova, Valery Bykovsky, Andriyan Nikolaev, and Pavel Popovich. These cosmonauts were eager to pilot the spacecrafts themselves.*

However, the designers wanted to prevent the cosmonaut from needlessly toying with the manual controls. So the designers built a special system. The instrument panel could be switched on only by turning a special combination lock.

If the ground control systems failed, Gagarin could find the numbers to the combination in a sealed envelope attached to the cabin wall. Gagarin's numbers were 1-4-5.

The designers felt that this system would lessen the cosmonaut's temptation to pilot the spacecraft. But it did make control available in case of emergency.

Gagarin never needed to open the envelope. The automatic systems worked perfectly. He was almost disappointed he did not get a chance to maneuver the craft in space.[8]

Vostok 1 continued through the darkness. After more than forty minutes Gagarin saw a halo appear around the edge of the Earth ahead of him. The sun then appeared brightly and suddenly over the horizon. He was flying into the bright side of the Earth again.

The flight so far was a complete success. Everything in the spacecraft was working well. Gagarin felt no discomfort from weightlessness. He had no trouble working in space.

The ship was passing over Africa as it flew into the sunlight. Gagarin knew the flight was almost over. It was almost time for the retro-rockets to be fired.

The retro-rockets would slow down the spacecraft and make it fall out of orbit. Its descent toward Earth would begin shortly after. The ship would begin falling toward Earth with great speed. This speed would be so great that the ship's friction with Earth's atmosphere would cause the ship's surface to grow red-hot.

Gagarin had completed his orbit and sent down much information about the experience of spaceflight. But the most dangerous part of the mission was yet to come. If the heatshield surface failed during reentry, Gagarin would be burned to dust. The design had worked in earlier unmanned test flights. But there was always the chance something could go wrong.

Gagarin, aboard Vostok 1, *had successfully completed one orbit, but was about to face the most dangerous part of the mission—reentry.*

At about 10:20 A.M. Moscow time, Gagarin felt *Vostok 1* turn slowly around. In a few moments the spacecraft had turned until he was facing backward from his flight path. Now he was in position for the retro-rockets to fire and slow the spacecraft.

If they fired, he would drop out of orbit and reentry would begin. If they did not fire, he would stay in orbit for ten days. After that period, Earth's gravity would finally pull the ship from orbit. The spacecraft did not carry enough supplies to keep Gagarin alive for that long.

The rockets had to work, or he would die. If the retro-rockets fired successfully, the heatshield had to work. If the heatshield failed, he also would die.

His flight had gone very smoothly so far. But there were still two very big hurdles to get over.

Gagarin, the men in the control room, and the Russian people listening on radio, waited as the moment for retrofire approached.

3

Reentry

Gagarin waited for the rockets to fire as he flew over central Africa. He was one hundred and twenty miles above Earth, and still 4,500 miles from his planned landing area.

At 10:20 A.M. Moscow time, the retro-rockets fired perfectly. There was a great sigh of relief in the control room. Gravity again settled over Yuri Gagarin's body. The first human in space was no longer in orbit. Gagarin and *Vostok 1* were headed downward in a long arc toward the Soviet Union.

The retro-rockets had now spent their fuel. The cone-shaped part of the ship that contained the retro-rockets separated from the spherical part that held Gagarin. Now only the spherical section was left. Gagarin and his ship were ready for reentry.

Several minutes later, the outside of the sphere began to get hot. The ship's friction with Earth's atmosphere greatly slowed the craft's speed. The rapid drop in speed pushed Gagarin's body deep into his couch. The effect on his body was the same as he had experienced during the rapid acceleration of liftoff.

The special heatshield surface grew hotter and hotter. Parts of the shield burned away the way its designers intended it to. When these chunks burned away from the ship, they also carried away the heat. This "burn away" process made the heat leave the ship. In that way the heat would not build up and heat the spacecraft to a temperature that would melt the ship and burn the cosmonaut.

Still, the stream of burning chunks created quite a fireworks display outside Gagarin's window. He would not know whether the reentry was going well until it was over. He could not know for sure that what was flaming past his window was supposed to be.

The fiery reentry continued for several minutes. During this time there was no radio contact between Gagarin and the control room. The heat of the reentry friction created a barrier to all radio signals.

Those minutes ticked by slowly for the men in the control room. They would not know of Gagarin's condition until his voice emerged from the radio blackout. So they waited.

And waited.

Vostok's heatshield, designed by people such as Sergei Korolev, was made to burn away. Here, Gagarin and Korolev meet.

Suddenly Gagarin's voice came through. He was all right. And the fiery phase of the reentry was over.

The spacecraft was now in a free fall. At about 20,000 feet, Gagarin and his couch ejected from the ship. Gagarin and the spacecraft fell separately to Earth. A parachute deployed from the top of the couch moments later. Then a drogue parachute shot out from the ship to steady its fall. A minute later its main parachute deployed. This slowed the spacecraft's descent. It drifted the remaining mile and a half to the ground.[1]

Finally, Gagarin deployed his own parachute and separated from the ejection couch. He too drifted toward the ground, landing near his spacecraft.

Yuri Gagarin returned to Earth with a jarring thud. He landed well within the planned recovery area, one hour and forty-eight minutes after liftoff. He and the spacecraft landed in a field near Smedlovka, a village four hundred miles southeast of Moscow.

The first thing Gagarin saw was a cow standing nearby. He got to his feet and gathered up his parachute. Then he noticed an older woman and two

One hour and forty-eight minutes after liftoff, Gagarin and the spaceship landed in a field in the Soviet Union.

young girls approaching him. The older woman, Anya Takhtarova, was the first to speak to him.

"Have you come from outer space?" she stammered. Gagarin was no doubt quite a sight in his bright orange coveralls and large white helmet.

"Yes!" Gagarin said triumphantly. "Would you believe it? I certainly have." The woman suddenly looked very frightened. Yuri then wondered if she thought he was from another country. Or perhaps another planet!

"Don't be alarmed," he said quickly, "I'm Soviet!"[2] Then Mrs. Takhtarova and her two daughters, Natasha and Rita, walked over with Gagarin to the ship. It was still smoking from reentry.

Minutes later a group of excited farmers were driving their tractors toward the landing site. Some of them had been listening to the radio. They knew the identity of the man who had just fallen from the sky into their field. They knew he had come all the way from space.

"Yuri Gagarin! Yuri Gagarin!" some of them shouted. Others helped him out of his coveralls.[3]

A recovery team went to pick him up in a helicopter. U.S. spacecrafts came down in the water, but all Soviet spaceships came down on land within the Soviet Union. The Soviets were afraid that the United States or some other country would recover and study their spaceships if the ships splashed down at sea.

One of the farmers gave Gagarin a cap to wear while he waited to be picked up by the helicopter recovery team. The ship was sending out a homing signal to help the recovery team locate him.

But it was unnecessary. The air base had already received a telephone call from a nearby village: "Gagarin is here."[4]

4

The Soviet Hero

When the helicopter landed, some of the landing support team gave Gagarin a brief checkup. Others began to work on the spacecraft. Soon Gagarin stepped into the helicopter and was flown to the nearby city of Saratov, along the Volga River. He would rest there and get a full medical examination.

When he arrived at Saratov, Gagarin was handed a telegram from Nikita Khrushchev, leader of the Soviet Union. "It gives me great joy to congratulate you warmly upon your spectacular heroic feat," the telegram said. Later, Khrushchev telephoned to speak directly to Gagarin.

"I shall be happy to meet you in Moscow," Khrushchev told him. "You and I, together with our whole people, shall celebrate this great exploit in the conquest of space."[1]

Two days later Gagarin was the focus of a hero's welcome unlike any Russia had ever seen. The joyous celebration in Moscow's Red Square was televised all over Europe. It was also taped for broadcast later to the rest of the world.

An American correspondent in Moscow reported:

> Weeping with emotion, Premier Khrushchev brought spaceman Yuri Gagarin home to Moscow Friday and the city's millions hailed the astronaut as the space-age Columbus in a roaring welcome. . . . Foreign

Valya and Yuri Gagarin meet with Nikita Khrushchev, the leader of the Soviet Union, and his wife, Nina, at a reception in the Kremlin Palace.

observers presumed that never in the 805-year-old history of Moscow has there been such an outpouring of public emotion.[2]

Another reporter wrote:

Pictures of Gagarin suddenly appeared on postcards and in blow-ups stuck all over the city. The Soviet government, which had jumped Gagarin from senior lieutenant to major just before the flight, now pinned on his chest its highest medal—Hero of the Soviet Union, and created a new title for him—pilot-cosmonaut.[3]

The celebration in Red Square lasted for hours. It was then followed by a reception in the Grand Kremlin Palace. The following day Gagarin answered questions at a news conference attended by a thousand reporters.

Many times Gagarin could not give answers to the reporters' questions. The Soviet Union at that time had a government that kept many secrets from the world, and from its own citizens.

Soviet leaders knew the United States was getting ready to put its first astronaut in space. So the Soviet government did not let Gagarin answer questions that might give information helpful to the United States and its space program.

The United States and the Soviet Union were in a "space race." The governments of both countries wanted to be both the first and the best in space achievements. Leaders from both governments

Yuri Gagarin became a hero after his flight. His name and face were everywhere. Here, his mother holds a Soviet magazine with Gagarin's name and photo on the cover.

believed that space accomplishments brought prestige and respect to their countries.

Many people in the United States were disappointed that the Soviet Union had put the first person in space. But the event was so historic it went beyond politics.

From earliest times, mankind had dreamed of going to the stars. On April 12, 1961, Yuri Gagarin had done it.

Gagarin is greeted by a cheering crowd of Soviet citizens in Red Square in Moscow.

Overnight he had become a national hero to the Soviet people. But his accomplishment also had captured the imagination of the world.

The world wanted to see him. The Soviet government was anxious and happy to have the world meet the first person in space, Yuri Gagarin.

5

Life of Yuri Gagarin

Gagarin traveled the world for months after his flight. He was met everywhere by large cheering crowds. The world's leaders gave him their highest honors for bravery and service to mankind. His handsome smile and pleasant personality made him appealing to people everywhere. His fame grew to be enormous. He became a legend in his own time.

He enjoyed his celebrity. But Gagarin was soon ready to get back to work. He had been a hard worker all his life.

Gagarin was born on March 9, 1934, in the Russian village of Klushino, about one hundred miles west of Moscow in the Smolensk region. He was the son of a carpenter. He attended primary school until the Germans invaded Russia in 1941. The schools did not reopen until 1945.

Gagarin later attended the Technical College at Gziatsk, near Moscow, and received his degree in 1951. He then moved to Saratov on the Volga River in southeastern Russia to attend the Industrial Technical College. He specialized in metalwork. While he was studying there, he joined the Aero Club and took his first solo flight in 1955.

After his flight, Gagarin traveled the world and his fame spread to many countries, but he was especially loved by the people of the Soviet Union. He delivered speeches to huge crowds, such as this one in Lenin Square.

Yuri Gagarin at age ten.

Yuri Gagarin was a pilot in the Soviet Air Force before he attained fame as a cosmonaut.

That same year he joined the Soviet Air Force and attended the Pilot Training College at Orenburg, near Russia's present eastern border with Kazakhstan. He completed fighter pilot training and made his first flight in a jet fighter in 1957. Two important events happened to Gagarin that year—he married his wife Valya, and the Soviet Union launched Sputnik, the world's first artificial satellite.

Gagarin learned in 1959 about the possibility of being trained for spaceflight. In early 1960 he applied to join the cosmonaut training program and his

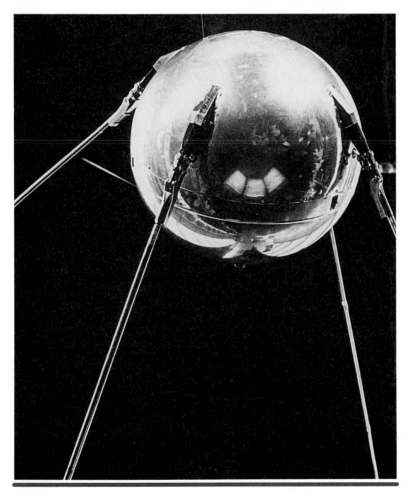

Sputnik was launched in 1957 by the Soviet Union. It was the world's first satellite.

application was accepted. The rest is indeed history.

After the world tour following his flight, Gagarin went back to work with the cosmonaut program. He graduated with honors from the Zhukovsky Air Force Academy and became Commander of the Cosmonaut's Detachment. In the years that followed, he yearned to get back into space.

"Being a cosmonaut is my profession," he said, "and I did not choose it just to make the first flight and then give it up."[1] He went back into regular cosmonaut training. In 1967 he was picked as backup pilot for the first flight of the newly developed *Soyuz* spacecraft.

The next year, sadly, tragedy struck.

On March 27, 1968, Yuri Gagarin was killed in a plane crash along with his training instructor. Millions in the Soviet Union mourned the loss of one of the greatest heroes in its history.

A year earlier, three American astronauts had died on the launchpad while training for the first Apollo mission. The risks of exploring space were high. The dangers claimed victims, no matter what flag they lived under. This time it had claimed humanity's first space traveler.

Yuri Gagarin believed that the competition for space achievement between the United States and the Soviet Union was good. He believed the competition would push the two countries to achieve greater things in space.

Following his flight, Gagarin told a reporter he was in favor "of a peaceful utilization of space and a peaceful competition. Of course we would rejoice in the successes of the American astronauts. There is space for all in the Universe."[2]

Yuri Gagarin's ashes were buried alongside other Soviet heroes in the Kremlin Wall. This great wall surrounds the main buildings of the Soviet government in Moscow. Gagarin had been such an appealing figure

Gagarin left behind a lasting legacy of heroism. Above, schoolchildren run on the grounds of the Soviet's space exploration center with a statue of Yuri Gagarin in the background.

to his fellow citizens. He was appealing because he took pride in the accomplishments of all Soviet people.

After his flight, he told the huge crowd gathered to meet him in Red Square: "One can say with assurance that on Soviet spacecraft we will fly even over more distant routes. I am boundlessly happy that my beloved homeland was the first to accomplish this flight, was the first to reach outer space . . ."[3]

CHAPTER NOTES

Chapter 1

1. Peter Smolders, *Soviets In Space* (New York: Taplinger Publishing Co., 1974), p. 110.

2. Shirley Thomas, *Men of Space* (Philadelphia: Chilton Company, 1961), p. 112.

3. Peter Bond, *Heroes in Space: From Gagarin to Challenger* (New York: Basil Blackwell Ltd., 1987), p. 14.

4. Smolders, p. 111.

5. Bond, p. 14.

6. Ibid., p. 15.

Chapter 2

1. Shirley Thomas, *Men of Space* (Philadelphia: Chilton Company, 1961), p. 113.

2. Ibid.

3. Peter Smolders, *Soviets In Space* (New York: Taplinger Publishing Co., 1974), p. 110.

4. Lloyd S. Swenson, James M. Grimwood, and Charles C. Alexander, *This New Ocean: The History of Project Mercury* (Washington, D.C.: National Aeronautics and Space Administration, 1966), p. 334.

5. *Pravda,* June 18, 1961.

6. Martin Caidin, *The Astronauts* (New York: E. P. Dutton and Company, 1961), p. 185.

7. Peter Bond, *Heroes in Space: From Gagarin to Challenger* (New York: Basil Blackwell Ltd., 1987), p. 15.

8. Ibid., p. 16.

Chapter 3

1. Phillip Clark, *The Soviet Manned Space Program* (New York: Salamander Books Ltd., 1988), p. 20.

2. Peter Bond, *Heroes in Space: From Gagarin to Challenger* (New York: Basil Blackwell Ltd., 1987), p. 12.

3. Ibid.

4. Shirley Thomas, *Men of Space* (Philadelphia: Chilton Co., 1961), p. 115.

Chapter 4

1. Peter Smolders, *Soviets In Space* (New York: Taplinger Publishing Co., 1974), p. 115.

2. Shirley Thomas, *Men of Space* (Philadelphia: Chilton Co., 1961), p. 117.

3. Ibid.

Chapter 5

1. Peter Bond, *Heroes in Space: From Gagarin to Challenger* (New York: Basil Blackwell Ltd., 1987), p. 17.

2. Peter Smolders, *Soviets In Space* (New York: Taplinger Publishing Co., 1974), p. 116.

3. Bond, p. 17.

GLOSSARY

cosmonaut—The name the Soviet space program gave to their space pilots. It comes from the Greek word *kosmos,* meaning "world" or "universe." The American name for space pilots, astronaut, comes from the Greek word *astron,* meaning "star."

Cosmonaut's Detachment—The Soviet space program's training group for space pilots. Yuri Gagarin was the leader of this group after his flight.

drogue parachute—A small parachute used to stabilize a falling object; it is also used to pull out a larger parachute from stowage.

G-forces—The force exerted on a body by gravity; also a measurement of how much additional force is being exerted on a body when it accelerates—a boy or girl who weighs one hundred pounds in 1-G (normal Earth gravity) will weigh two hundred pounds at 2-G acceleration.

heatshield—The surface that covers the reentry side of early spacecrafts. Parts of the surface were designed to burn away. This would carry the heat away, and prevent heat from building up on the spacecraft.

retro-rockets—Rockets that are fired near the end of a spaceflight to slow the ship down in preparation for reentry.

Union of Soviet Socialist Republics (USSR)—Name for the former communist government of Russia. This government controlled Russia and parts of eastern Europe from 1917 to 1991, when the Communist party in Russia collapsed.

Vostok—Name for the first series of Soviet manned spacecrafts. Because world maps are arranged with the United States to the west and the Soviet Union to the east, the Soviets named the spacecrafts *Vostok,* which means "east."

FURTHER READING

Bond, Peter. *Heroes in Space: From Gagarin to Challenger*. New York: Basil Blackwell Ltd., 1987.

Clark, Phillip. *The Soviet Manned Space Program*. New York: Salamander Books Ltd., 1988.

Prakasan, K. P. *Space - Gagarin & After*. New York: Apt Books, Inc., 1987.

Smolders, Peter. *Soviets in Space*. New York: Taplinger Publishing Co., 1974.

Thomas, Shirley. *Men of Space*. Philadelphia: Chilton Company, 1961.

INDEX

Vostok 1 : first human in
  space
Author: Cole, Michael D.
Reading Level: 5.5 MG
Point Value: 1.0
ACCELERATED READER QUIZ# 15666